emotions have no gender

Lauren McFarlane

Presentation by *BookLeaf Publishing*

Web: www.bookleafpub.com

E-mail: info@bookleafpub.com

ISBN: 9789357212632

First edition 2023

To all the great and beautiful men in my life...

PREFACE

Growing up I always saw the males in my life being strong and independent. They would always look out for me and want to protect me. As I've gotten older, I've noticed that I've returned that protection and been someone that these males have confided in. Mental health has no agenda and doesn't target someone based on their gender, I have lost male friends who lost their battle and took their lives prematurely. There needs to be a stop to the stigma that surrounds men's mental health. I've been inspired by those men in my life not only to write these pieces, but to share them. In no way do I consider myself a poet, but when I shared a quote with my Year Seven English group 'Thoughts that breathe and words that burn" they told me how this could be so true and that we could all share our thoughts if we put them in to words, so this is what I have done, in the hope that they reach someone in need.

acknowledge it

You're told to be strong and tough,

You're taught that men don't cry

and that you can't be weak.

"Man up"

Why are we trying to hide it?

Why doesn't society see it?

Why are men made out to be something else?

"Man up"

Acknowledge the fact that mental health is
health

Acknowledge that it isn't exclusive to one
gender

Acknowledge that we can all feel pain

"Man up"

The pain and trauma,

The demands and torment,

The agony and discomfort.

"Man up"

"Anything that's human is mentionable, and anything that is mentionable can be more manageable. When we can talk about our feelings, they become less overwhelming, less upsetting, and less scary." – Fred Rogers.

emotions have no gender

emotions have no gender

males and females alike in feelings

the human brain develops differently in genders

it isn't exclusive to one or the other

we all have the ability to feel pain

physically and mentally

we all have the ability to speak up,

only some choose not to

because their gender doesn't allow them to

bound by society's expectations

and not by the reality

girls will play with Barbies

and talk about how they feel

boys will play with cars

and mask how they feel

what happens when boys become men?

when men get sad?

when men are masking their feelings?

when men are opening up

they are shamed

they are labelled, weak

when does society learn,

emotions have no gender?

"Regardless of who you are or what you do for a
living or where you come from, it doesn't
discriminate. We all kind of go through it." –
Dwayne 'The Rock Johnson.

bend before you break

There is something to say for the importance of being able to talk to someone,

Whilst you can talk to people who are your friends and family, can you really talk to them?

It's okay that they don't always understand,

But it's important that you have someone you can talk to

Someone you can share your thoughts with

Someone you can go to when you need.

There's comfort in a stranger

Someone who doesn't know you

Someone who is impartial to what is going on in our life

There's no prejudice

There's no judgement

Because at the end of the day,

They only know what you tell them.

They have no preconceived ideas, no prior knowledge

They only know what you are telling them,

They only know what you are saying.

It's something we all need,

Someone to go to when you aren't feeling great

Just not feeling yourself

Someone you can lean on in times of need

But sometimes we forget the importance of this person

Using them to the fullest

Being our most vulnerable with them

We are our own worst enemy

Bottling up every thought, every emotion.

We continue to bottle these feelings,

Until eventually, we pop!

It's a coke bottle being shaken consistently

Every time we feel shaken,

Another 'dark' though

Another self-doubt

Another bottled emotion

The gas in the bottle builds and builds

Eventually we let some of it out,

But the bottle overflows.

The lid can't be put back

And we are left

Sat there

Pouring out all the build up of feelings

There is danger in the bottle imploding

And we mentally and physically crash

Or it explodes...

"The heart of man is very much like the sea; it
has its storms, it has its tides, and in its depths, it
has its pearls too." – Vincent Van Gogh, artist.

toxic mask of manliness

This world wrongly taught males to mask their emotions

The ideal man by society's standards is strong

Both physically and mentally

This is toxic

What if they don't fit the 'ideals' set by society?

Are they broken?

Are they wrong?

No

It is toxic to think we all fit the 'ideals' set by society

It will never be that way

But we need to teach men that they have been taught wrong

That society fails them

That the mask needs to be removed

Manliness is being strong, being weak, being vulnerable

But most of all

Being individual

Being unique

And being yourself

Owning your emotions

Your thoughts and feelings

So, drop the toxic mask of manliness set by society.

"Shoutout to all the men going through a lot, with no one to turn to, because this world wrongly taught men to mask their emotions."
—Unknown.

Past

We all have pasts

We have all made mistakes

We all made choices that maybe weren't the best
ones

We aren't all completely innocent

We are all unique though

And the thing about life is

If we are lucky,

We wake up everyday

With another chance

With a fresh start

To be better than the person we were yesterday

"It takes more courage to reveal insecurities than to hide them, more strength to relate to people than to dominate them, more 'manhood' to abide by thought-out principles rather than blind reflex. Toughness is in the soul and spirit, not in muscles and an immature mind." – Alex Karras.

Present

You wake up every day with a new opportunity.

You have each day to make a difference.

Stop waiting for the right moment.

Each day is a gift.

Grab life by the balls,

And take it,

Run with it.

Our greatest weapon,

Is our strength.

Our unique identity,

And our ability to adapt and overcome.

Make the most of the present,

And the time you have right now.

Future

No one knows what will happen tomorrow

No one knows what is going to happen in the next hour

We aren't guaranteed a future

Or another day

But we all have hopes and dreams

We all have talents and drive

Don't wait for tomorrow

Don't wait for the next day

Plant your feet

Or set them free

Just don't wait,

Because tomorrow isn't guaranteed.

No one else can feel it for you

Strength is not the absence of weakness,
but rather the ability to rise from adversity,
impacted but not destroyed.

You cannot fail the journey you are on.
You own it, it's yours -
mistakes, flaws, differences, trauma and
obstacles.
All these things make you think you are failing
the journey at some point,
but if you learn from this,
rise from the low points,
get your shit together
and pick up the pieces,
you continue your journey and just become
stronger because of it.

Most people are afraid,
or give up when they hit a rough patch,
or feel failure during their journey -
this is generally because we are ingrained to
think and believe that failing,
making mistakes, or trauma is a bad thing.

Society has us believing that these things are all
looked down upon
and suffering is something that will just show
your weaknesses.

Deciding to let your mistakes,
pains, fails and obstacles get to you
and bring you down, creating a stop in your
journey is up to you.
Only you decide how any of this actually affects
your life.
Only you can let it in.

I'll be happy when...

Ultimately putting a price or object on happiness
"I'll be happy when..."
Why can't we be happy with what we have?
Why can we not just appreciate what is already
ours?
This "I'll be happy when I have this job, that car,
marriage, a child…"
Whatever it is that you are weighing your
happiness on,
is actually weighing you down.
Are you truly saying that you won't be happy
until those things happen?
You refuse to be happy until you look a certain
way,
you can't be happy unless you own that car or
have that job,
you cannot possibly be happy until you have
achieved your five-year plan?

The thing with thinking like this is that it buries
you,
because the finish line always moves.

Be happy with your life now,
with everything that you have.

Think about your health,
your abilities,
your knowledge,
your heart – everything you have in this moment
is something worth being happy about.
It is okay to think about the future,
and what will make you happy then,
but that's not a reason to not be happy in the
present moment.
You can look forward to things
and set goals and milestones to achieve –
but don't waste the time you have,
and the journey that you're on waiting for
something else.

The finish line always moves.

We go through life believing that there is more
to happiness,
that there is more to what will make us happy.
But take a look around you right now,
what is one thing that you are grateful for or
happy about?
It could be that you are grateful for your good
health
in a time of chaos in the world,
it could be for your friends and family,
it could be for your legs that are strong and
allow you to walk around all day,

it could be that you are grateful for your bed at
night.
All of these listed things can make you happy.
So why can't you be happy now?
Why is it that people still say "I'll be happy
when…"

The finish line always moves.

Happiness is a funny thing really.
It is within us,
but we look for it externally.
We look for others to make ourselves happy.
We look for materialistic things to bring us joy.

Challenge yourself now.
Think about all the things that you want to have
in six months' time.
What would make you really happy if you were
to have it in six months?
It can be anything,
from a new car,
a higher paying job,
your dream house,
to a stable relationship,
children and more money.
Now think about one thing you already have that
you are happy about.

Again, it can be anything,
but it has to be something that truly brings you
joy.
Now think,
if you weren't to get your six-month happiness
object/feeling,
would you be unhappy?
Would you forget about the current thing that is
making you happy because you didn't get what
you wanted?

The journey isn't a short one,
it is your whole life.
We often go through it just planning for the
future,
asking for wishes to come true,
setting happiness goals,
but living in the moment is different.
Knowing what you are happy for in this
moment,
will play a huge part in how you think about
your future.
Research has stated that practicing gratitude
each day makes us physically and mentally
stronger.
Don't get caught up in what will make you
happy,
think about what already makes you happy and
appreciate it.

Be grateful for the journey that you are on now.

The finish line always moves.

Ghosts

but that's exactly what happens
when someone leaves.
they become like ghosts,
because sometimes you can't see them,
but you could still feel them,
once they're gone.

sad things happen

this is why you have to keep going,
because sad things have to happen.
without them our lives would be meaningless.
a bird does not ask the sky to stop raining,
it will fly through the storm no matter what.

Your version of you

Everybody who knows of you has an idea of
you.

There are a thousand different versions of you
out there.
Every person you meet,
have a relationship with
or make eye contact with on the street
creates a 'version' of you.

The only person that you think of as 'yourself'
only exists for you.
In peoples minds the version of you will be
different,
depending on who they are,
not who you are.

People who use to know you -
will know the past you
and probably a version of you that doesn't exist
anymore.
But in their minds that is who you are.

Who you are depends on many things,
but truly no one knows the whole you.

What you do with this is up to you.

Manly

To let down a wall,
to shed a tear.
To feel exposed,
to open up.

Feeling exposed,
feeling vulnerable.
Feeling defenceless,
feeling sensitive.

To be unguarded,
to be liable.
To be unarmed,
to be unfortified.

Feeling assailable,
feeling susceptible.
Feeling weak,
feeling unguarded.

To cry,
to open up.
To love
and be loved.

That's manly.

"Ultimate vulnerability. That's manly." –
Cameron Conaway

When the thoughts in our head aren't our own.   Told for years one thing so you believe it.

Do you ever think about something so much,

that you don't know why you started thinking about it in the first place?

Sometimes it can be that another person has put these thoughts in to your head.

Often what we think of ourselves

and how we perceive ourselves,

is another person's thoughts.

These ideas get stuck in our minds and somewhat become our own ideas.

We a fed so much bullshit in our lives that,

we take it all in and believe it's truth.

This ends up being a cyclone of emotion

and ill truth that generally doesn't fit our lives.

It isn't until we turn around,

do something for ourselves

that we realise we have been absorbing everyone
else's ideas and perceptions of the world,

we let it become our own.

Are the thoughts currently in your head, your
own?

It is something worth thinking about.

You know how everyone has a voice?

How much of your own voice is actually your
voice?

How easily influenced are you by what someone
else says?

Sometimes the bullshit we hear over and over
again

about ourselves gets stuck inside our heads and
we believe it

for so long that it becomes really difficult to
change that.

You believe that if someone told you for years
that you weren't good enough,

or that you wouldn't be able to follow your
dreams,

or even that you wouldn't amount to anything.

What changes this?

How do we get stuck in this mind frame?

too short

Life is too short for half-hearted promises and
reluctant involvements.
You need to believe in what you're doing,
to feel sure of what you're a part of
and to be clear about what you don't want.

You Own It

You are not your thoughts.
Your thoughts do not define you.
Your mind doesn't own you.
You own it.
Treat it with respect and love.
The same way you treat those you care about.
Respect that you are good enough.

Brave

You're brave
because life gives you every reason to want to
give up
and still, you rise
You pick yourself up and carry on.
If you're not where you want to be in life,
keep going.
If you don't examine your fears,
they will control you for the rest of your life.
Sometimes,
you have to be brave
and a little wild,
and just say,
"fuck it; I trust myself; let's see what happens".
Treat yourself like you're the closest friend
you've got.
Celebrate the magnificent creature that you are.
Don't let anyone mess with you,
your dreams,
least of all yourself.

"I deserve to have peace. I deserve to be happy
and smiling. Why not me? I guess I give so
much of myself to others I forget that I need to
show myself some love too. I think I never

really knew how. I'm scared, I'm sad, I feel like
I let a lot of people down, and again, I'm sorry.
It's time I fix me. I'm nervous, but ima get
through this." - Kid Cudi.

your choice

sometimes you need to set yourself a challenge
it could be anything from chasing a dream,
to moving away.
sometimes you need to set yourself free from a
burden,
sometimes that burden is a toxic relationship,
a difficult place,
a shit job or just a negative mindset.
we outgrow things and become tired of being
caught up on the same rollercoaster
again and again.
but by being human we learn to adapt and grow
through the shit
people change,
people leave.
you don't have control over that,
and whilst it might drive you crazy, it's reality.
you might loose your mind a little bit along the
way,
but you get wiser and start focusing your energy
differently,
what you give,
and what you let in, changes.
and it's your choice.

rulers of our own destiny

the unconscious mind drives a lot of our
behaviour.
it is where we hold our thoughts,
memories, urges and emotions.
these are all things that could be positive or
negative,
could be happy or sad,
the memories you've repressed,
the urges you once had,
and emotions you've ridden through.
think about that for a minute.
if our unconscious mind is where we hold a lot
of these feelings
and we allow it to drive a lot of our behaviour
and attitude
the consequences could ultimately be up to us
be wary of where your unconscious mind drives
you

Unique Silence

there's something about silence that many people
don't get,
and there are many types of silence.
people can be silent in times of grace,
in times of gratitude, solitude, contemplation,
prayer, reflection or meditation.
there's a unique silence that people also have,
used in times when usually only they will
understand.
if they are lucky enough they might have
someone around that notices
and begins to recognise that unique silence.
the ability to understand and use non-verbal
communication
or body language is a powerful tool.

silence can yield more power than words.

There's something about someone that
understands unique silence.

Belief

'Belief is half of all healing.
Belief in the cure,
belief in the future that awaits'.

What do you believe in?
How do you know what to believe in?
People often say "if you just believe..."
but for every person that does believe,
it seems that there's a person that doesn't
and just says "that's rubbish..."
So what do those people believe?

Your reality is a reflection of your strongest
belief.
What you do,
what you believe,
what you accept as standard,
what you put in out in to the universe,
will ultimately reflect in your reality.